ALFRED NOBEL

and the Story of the Nobel Prize

GREAT ACHIEVEMENT
A · W · A · R · D · S

Mitchell Lane
PUBLISHERS

P.O. Box 196
Hockessin, Delaware 19707

GREAT ACHIEVEMENT
A·W·A·R·D·S

Titles in the Series

Visit us on the web at www.mitchelllane.com
Comments? Email us at mitchelllane@mitchelllane.com

ALFRED NOBEL

and the Story of the Nobel Prize

GREAT ACHIEVEMENT

A · W · A · R · D · S

Printing   2   3   4   5   6   7   8   9
Library of Congress Cataloging-in-Publication Data
Bankston, John, 1974-
    Alfred Nobel and the story of the Nobel Prize / by John Bankston.
        p. cm. — (Great achievement awards)
    Summary: A biography of the reclusive inventor of dynamite and the story of how he came to establish the prestigious prizes that bear his name.
    Includes bibliographical references and index.
    ISBN 1-58415-168-4 (library)
        1. Nobel, Alfred Bernhard, 1833-1896—Juvenile literature. 2. Nobel Prizes—History—Juvenile literature. 3. Philanthropists—Sweden—Biography—Juvenile literature. 4. Chemical engineers—Sweden—Biography—Juvenile literature. [1. Nobel, Alfred Bernhard, 1833-1896. 2. Chemical Engineers. 3. Nobel Prizes—History.] I. Title. II. Series.
AS911.N9 B36 2002
001.4'4—dc21   2002069453

ABOUT THE AUTHOR: Born in Boston, Massachusetts, John Bankston has written over three dozen biographies for young adults profiling scientists like Jonas Salk and Alexander Fleming, celebrities like Mandy Moore and Alicia Keys, great achievers like Coretta Scott King, and master musicians like Franz Peter Schubert and Wolfgang Amadeus Mozart. An avid reader and writer, he has worked in Los Angeles, California as a producer, screenwriter and actor. Currently he is in pre-production on *Dancing at the Edge*, a semi-autobiographical film he hopes to film in Portland, Oregon. Last year he completed his first young adult novel, *18 to Look Younger*.

PHOTO CREDITS: Cover: The Nobel Foundation; p. 6 Corbis; p. 8 Hulton/Archive; p. 10 The Nobel Foundation; p. 16 Christel Gerstenberg/Corbis; p. 20 The Nobel Foundation; p. 22 The Nobel Foundation; p. 24 Archivo Iconografico, S.A./Corbis; p. 28 Lynda Richardson/Corbis; p. 32 The Nobel Foundation; p. 34 The Nobel Foundation; p. 35 Getty Images; p. 38 Ted Spiegel/Corbis; p. 40 Getty Images

PUBLISHER'S NOTE: The following story has been thoroughly researched and to the best of our knowledge represents a true story. Documentation of such research can be found on page 46.

The web sites referenced in this book were all active as of the publication date. Because of the fleeting nature of some internet sites, we cannot guarantee they will be active when you are reading this book.

TABLE OF CONTENTS

Nobel and dynamite earned their bad reputations in part because of cartoons like this one published in 1884. Despite dynamite's risks, its use helped fuel the industrial revolution.

would save many more lives than it cost. About eighty years before the atomic bomb was developed, Alfred Nobel believed his invention had that kind of potential. The gunpowder–nitroglycerin combination he developed was used in land mines and for bombs constructed by anarchists who wanted to overthrow their governments. But Nobel believed that his dynamite and the ever more powerful explosives that followed would eventually be a deterrent. "My factories may make an end to war sooner than your congresses," Nobel once stated. "The day when two Army corps can annihilate each other in one second, all civilized nations, it is hoped, will recoil from war and discharge their troops."

Besides, dynamite served many purposes other than warfare. It was used by railroad engineers to blast tunnels through mountains. It sped the construction of mines and made it easier to extract precious resources such as gold and coal from the earth. Its invention spurred the Industrial Revolution, the period starting in the late 1700s when developed countries such as England and the United States moved from economies based on farming to ones based on manufacturing.

Dynamite, probably more than any other substance developed in the nineteenth century, paved the way for modernization. Yet as Alfred Nobel considered the French obituary, he realized he needed to make changes. He was near the end of his life. When his real obituary was published, he did not want it to describe him with phrases like "merchant of death." He wanted to leave something behind. He wanted to reward those who work for peace, because many thought his invention was used to start wars.

In 1888, Alfred Nobel had been given an incredible opportunity. How many people get to "see" their own death? How many get a second chance at a brand-new life? Nobel's choice was like the one offered forty-five years before to fictional miser Ebenezer Scrooge in the famous Charles Dickens novel *A Christmas Carol*. Scrooge was visited by three ghosts who showed him his past, his present, and his future. Distressed by what he saw, he chose to change his life and help the less fortunate. After reading the obituary, Alfred Nobel had a pretty good idea of how others viewed his past and his present. The only question was the future. What was he going to do about it?

An "explosive" demonstration for the Russian Czar by Immanuel Nobel proves how effective the mines he built could be.

SURVIVAL

I n the 1830s, the Nobel family was suffering through hard times. Succeeding despite tremendous obstacles was a legacy—for generations the Nobels' achievements had been accomplished with little formal education or personal wealth. Immanuel Nobel, Alfred's father, was just one in a long line of such men.

In the 1600s, Peder Olufsson took the name of his hometown, Ostra Nobbelov, becoming Petrus Nobelius. He was the first "Nobel" and gained success as a judge, despite his lack of education in law. His grandson studied at medical school but likewise never earned a degree. He still became a prominent hospital physician.

The Nobels could look with pride upon many family accomplishments; unfortunately, holding on to money was never one of them. Immanuel Nobel was born into poverty and forced to drop out of school when he was fourteen. He worked as a cabin boy for several years, traveling across the world before returning to Sweden and attending the Academy of Liberal Arts as an architecture student. He learned a great deal about buildings, but there were gaps in Immanuel's education that always embarrassed him. He read widely in his free time, trying to make up for his lack of a classical education.

Immanuel became a successful builder. He also set up Sweden's first rubber factory, supplying the military and hospitals. As his income increased, he moved his young wife, Andriette, and two sons, Ludvig and Robert, into a series of middle-class homes. With each new home, a child was born. Although Immanuel and Andriette also had to cope with tragedy—several of their children died in infancy—they had a happy marriage and prosperous life.

In the 1830s, all of that changed.

Three barges Immanuel owned sank, taking with them tons of expensive building materials that he had to pay for. A project he was working on collapsed, forcing him to rebuild at his own expense.

And then the family home burned down.

Although Andriette was able to rescue the children (Immanuel was not home at the time), everything they owned was lost. The family relocated to a shabby apartment, and they struggled to make ends meet. Despite his best efforts, Immanuel could not do it. In the beginning of 1833, Immanuel Nobel declared bankruptcy, which provided legal protection against his creditors while he tried to get his life back together.

Ten months later, Alfred was born.

Alfred Bernhard Nobel came into the world on October 21, 1833. Just as his father had thirty-two years before, the infant grew up in crushing poverty.

Alfred's early years were spent in the cramped rooms of the Nobels' second-floor apartment in the northern end of Stockholm, Sweden. Relying on a woodstove for heat, they were often freezing: the thin walls offered little protection from arctic winds that swept across the country. In the early morning, working by oil lamps, which slowly filled the room with thick black smoke, Andriette, a seamstress, would tackle her sewing. She would make clothes for her children from whatever scraps of fabric she could scrounge up from the jobs she took. Immanuel was as much a dreamer as an inventor; for several years he earned very little money. The family struggled. Andriette often had to ask her father, a successful accountant, for a few kroner (less than a dollar) to feed her children.

Outside the Nobels' small apartment, life for Stockholm's poor was very difficult. The streets and alleys served as dumping grounds for garbage cans and household privies (toilets). Rats ran wild, and many of the town's residents contracted a variety of diseases, including diphtheria, cholera, and whooping cough. Still, Immanuel never abandoned his dreams. He invented land and sea mines, incorporating the same type of rubber his factory had produced. He tried to interest the Swedish military in his new devices. They just weren't interested.

At home, Alfred was a sickly child, suffering from persistent infections. His mother, who had seen several of her children die by the time Alfred was born, doted on her son more than her other, healthier, boys. "My cradle looked like a deathbed," Alfred wrote in a poem when he was eighteen, "and for years a mother watched with ever anxious care."

Around the time Alfred was four, Immanuel met Lars Gabriel von Haartman, the governor of Turku, Finland, at a party. The governor oversaw a Russian organization that brought foreign business interests into the country. Immanuel described the research he had done with land mines. Before the party ended, Lars invited the elder Nobel to come to Turku and work. Immanuel had nothing to lose.

On December 4, 1837, Immanuel boarded a ship and waved good-bye to his family. They would not see him for another five years.

Immanuel Nobel had never been the family breadwinner, and in his absence, Andriette did everything she could to keep her children fed and clothed. With loans from relatives, she set up a small store that sold vegetables and milk. Alfred, Ludvig, and Robert sold matches on street corners. From a young age the Nobel children learned the value of money—a lesson they would never forget.

"One of my most painful memories is a little episode from this time," Robert was quoted by biographer Erik Bergengren in *Alfred Nobel: The Man and His Work,* "when I had been sent out by my mother to buy food for dinner with a three penny bit, and I lost the pitiful little coin."

School, when Alfred was healthy enough to attend, offered some respite. He began going to the Jacob Parish Apologist School when he was seven. The school offered a low-cost education for poor children. It was a harsh place, where students were disciplined with carpet beaters, and poor ventilation often caused the rooms to fill with smoke from the oil lamps and a small woodstove. Still, Alfred owned an inquisitive mind and did well academically, earning As and Bs in subjects like Power of Comprehension and Manners.

His mother often wrote to Immanuel, who was justifiably proud of his frail son. He described Alfred in one letter as "my good and industrious son highly valued both by his parents and his brothers for his knowledge as well as for his untiring work ability, which nothing can replace."

This belief of Immanuel's, that hard work was more important than anything, was a philosophy shared by his son. Although Alfred and his father clashed over many other issues, this was one topic upon which both could agree. While Alfred was putting in two arduous semesters at Jacob Parish, his father moved from Turku to St. Petersburg, Russia. The country, then under the rule of a czar (like a king), was actively recruiting businesspeople and inventors from other countries. Immanuel was able to set up an engineering workshop, Ogareff and Nobel's Authorized Foundry and Wheel Factory. By 1842 he'd saved enough money to send for his family.

The factory specialized in land and sea mines, gun carriages, and machine tools. The business was fairly prosperous—when his wife and three sons arrived in St. Petersburg, Immanuel was able to move them into a solid, middle-class house. It was much nicer than the one they had had in Sweden, but just as drafty.

Freezing temperatures were just about the only thing St. Petersburg had in common with Stockholm. The new family home was one story, not terribly large, and somewhat rundown, but it provided a scenic view of a St. Petersburg canal.

Andriette moved into her new home, and within a year, their son Emil was born. He was the last child the couple would have to survive past infancy.

Andriette and Immanuel doted on Emil even more than they had Alfred, who was a decade older. Because he was so much younger than the other three boys, Emil was definitely the baby of the family, and his siblings looked out for him.

Thanks to his father's industry, Alfred and his two older brothers did not have to suffer in an unpleasant classroom, as they had in Sweden. Instead, Immanuel hired a number of well-educated private tutors for his offspring, including B. Lars Santesson, who taught Swedish language and history, and Nikolaj Zinin, a Russian chemist who provided Alfred with a strong grounding in the sciences. Professor Zinin would eventually change Alfred's life.

As a teen, however, it was not science but language that fascinated Alfred. In addition to Swedish he studied English, Italian, German, and

French. Eventually he would achieve such fluency that, unlike many wealthy men, he wrote his own letters—he could not trust a secretary to handle the translations.

When he reached seventeen his talent in five languages served an immediate purpose. *Travel.* Alfred's father believed that seeing a wider part of the world would provide more of an education for his son than any tutor or classroom. In 1849, young Alfred boarded a ship, ready for a journey that would take him across Europe and, eventually, to the United States.

Item am puchsen ma[?]*louch vnd recht laden So such an d erst daz daz puluer*
gut sey Ttm nyn an moz vnd stoz sie in die puchsen vnd tail die moz geleich in
fünf tail also an derfigur wol sichst vnd lad die vn wil mit puluer als die moz
saget/ so ist si mit puluer recht geladen wann d kloz bedekf sein wart/ So sol d puluer
vnd kloz vnd dem puluer auch am wart sein, daz daz feur zu recht prunst vnd auch
zu recht kraft mag komen. Item darnach machtu dan amen kloz vnd ainen stain daz
paz schiessen.

Gunpowder, the main ingredient in Nobel's inventions, has existed for centuries as this illustration from a manuscript published around the 15th century proves.

FOREIGN LANDS

Most of Alfred's journeys as a teenager went unrecorded, but as an older man he wrote a poem illustrating how he felt when he first leaned over the railing of a ship and peered across the vastness of the Atlantic Ocean. "I left in early youth my home for distant lands beyond the sea, but strange to say, even when the Ocean spread its grandeur 'round, it struck me not as new—my mind had pictured Oceans far more wide."

Alfred's imagination was as big as any ocean. For Immanuel, that was a problem. From the time he was a kid, Alfred retreated to the worlds of poetry, stories, and plays. He read and wrote in Swedish, in English, in all of the languages he studied. Teachers and other professionals who read his work were generally impressed by his talent and encouraged him to pursue his dreams. As a youth, Alfred considered a career as a writer.

The concept disgusted Immanuel. He did not want some idle dreamer for a son. Immanuel believed in industry, in manufacturing—in what was *real,* not what went on in a writer's head. Immanuel loved to read, but to him the occupation of writer was disreputable. It wasn't honest work.

Alfred was not a rebellious teen. He realized the travels his father was willing to finance came with strings attached. His trips to France and Italy, journeys made by many famous authors over the last two centuries, were not designed to help him become more artistic.

By the late 1840s, Immanuel's business producing land and sea mines was booming. Yet he realized how inefficient an explosive gunpowder was for his needs. Gunpowder, a Chinese invention, was by then over eight hundred years old, and Immanuel suspected there was something better. So, while he paid for Alfred's trip, it was not designed as a casual tour. It was business.

What Alfred would be doing was a form of apprenticeship. Just as young people worked for blacksmiths and carpenters in hopes of learning a trade, Immanuel expected his son to study with engineers and chemists so that he could become one. Alfred would need engineering and chemistry skills to work in the Nobel factory.

In the summer of 1849, Alfred traveled from St. Petersburg to Sweden. Because there were few trains operating in Russia, his trek was made by horse and carriage—a demanding and unpleasant trip over rough and ruined roads.

Once in Sweden he stayed with older brother Ludvig, who in a letter to his father wrote, "Alfred has grown so much that I hardly knew him. He is almost as tall as I am and his voice is so deep and gruff that I should hardly have recognized him by it."

At seventeen, Alfred was shorter than the average nineteenth-century man, but his build was compact and solid. Photos from the time reveal a teenager with dark and casual hair, his long bangs falling over a serious forehead. With his wide mouth and long eyelashes, he was considered attractive by many women, but for his entire life Alfred despised the way he looked. Indeed, as he got older he wore a thick beard. Although it was the fashion of the time, Alfred was probably grateful for the way the hair hid his face.

Relying on his father's business connections, Alfred traveled to England and Germany. Only his trip to Italy was for pleasure alone—the country at the time offered few benefits for an aspiring engineer but certainly fed the creative and troubled soul Alfred often described in his writings. As he put it in *Nemesis,* a semiautobiographical play he composed, "Thus I grew into a thinking and feeling creature with an innerworld of poetry that no tyranny has been able to extirpate [destroy]."

After his trip through Italy, Alfred went to France. In the nineteenth century, Paris was considered by many to be the most cosmopolitan, modern, and exciting city of all the great cities in the world. Alfred certainly agreed with this opinion, later describing Paris as "an ocean where Passion creates stormy weather and causes more wrecks than ever the salty waves did."

Alone and with few resources when he arrived, there was little opportunity for Alfred to negotiate the "Passion" he described. Instead he began studying with a famous chemist referred to only as Professor Pelouze. Pelouze had established a free laboratory in 1846; students arrived in Paris from all over the world, eager to learn. By this time, Alfred was already an accomplished chemist, thanks to the education provided by Zinin. Still, Pelouze's free lab provided a unique and fortunate opportunity: as a foreigner without a diploma, Alfred would never have been admitted to a French university.

After Paris, New York was a disappointment.

Alfred Nobel left the City of Light on a transatlantic journey, which by the 1850s was common but still quite difficult. For the most part steamships had replaced sailing vessels, and the crossing's time was reduced from over three weeks to around ten days.

Speed came with a price, however, as much of the ship's space was devoted to the equipment needed to run it. Steamers were far more cramped and noisy than sailing ships. And after the celebratory first day at sea, meals consisted of salty beef and fish—day in and day out. Hardly a first-class passenger, Alfred's budget-conscious father most likely purchased the cheapest ticket possible. At the time, third-class passengers slept on hard benches with thin mattresses in large rooms, a sheer curtain providing little privacy. On the entire ship there were only a few bathrooms serving hundreds of travelers.

There was no hot water.

Even first-class passengers suffered. Author Charles Dickens, both rich and famous by the time of his transatlantic crossing in 1842, wrote that his cabin was a "preposterous box," and the luggage he brought could "no more be got in the door . . . than a giraffe could be persuaded or forced into a flower pot." Dickens went on to describe the first-class dining room as "not unlike a gigantic hearse with windows on the sides."

It is interesting that Alfred Nobel's primary goal when he journeyed to the United States was to meet with John Ericsson. The fellow Swede and shipbuilder gained notice when he developed a propeller-powered ship. Ericsson tested the device when he took just such a vessel across the ocean in 1838. In the 1850s, the propeller-driven ship would begin to replace ones powered by paddle wheels, like the one Alfred took.

An attractive youth, Nobel hated the way he looked and dreamed of being a writer.

To Alfred's eyes, New York City must have seemed a tremendous letdown after the beauty of Paris. Far from the modern, cosmopolitan city it is now, New York City and particularly the borough of Manhattan in the

1850s was a grim and crowded place. Rundown in the poorer sections, the streets were as dirty and waste-filled as the Stockholm slum. North of 42nd Street, in what is now Times Square, New York was rural, used mainly for farmland and agriculture.

Poet Walt Whitman, a newspaper reporter when Alfred arrived in the city described the isle of Manhattan as "sterile and sandy, on a foundation of rock it was not an inviting place, but bleak."

Also at that time, Ericsson's work was focused on developing and refining the warm air engine. By 1850 he had sold over 12,000 of the units in New York City alone. Immanuel knew an opportunity when he saw one; he hoped Alfred would learn how to manufacture the device and convince Ericsson to let them produce them in Russia and Europe.

Alfred wrote very little about his time at Ericsson's three-story house at 36 Beach Street, but the shipbuilder's influence was obvious. By the time Alfred returned to St. Petersburg, he no longer wanted to be an engineer or a chemist. He wanted to be an inventor.

In 1862, the Confederate Army's *Merrimac* was thwarted in its approach to Virginia's coast by the Union Army's *Monitor.* The Union's iron-plated warship had been constructed by John Ericsson, and the four-hour battle waged by the two vessels became one of the most famous conflicts in maritime history. It also brought the Swedish shipbuilder worldwide fame.

Alfred Nobel would gain similar wealth and fame with an invention used in warfare. But when Alfred arrived back home in Russia after years of travel, he found that his father was already getting rich from wartime profits.

By the 1880s, Nobel was fabulously wealthy but still very unhappy. He never married and his only known relationship was with a young woman who seemed to only love his money.

THE PRICE OF WAR

At six years old, Immanuel Nobel constructed a simple prism from a piece of ice. It was his first invention. His genius for innovation was inherited by Alfred, who a few years after returning home applied for his first patent. The patent ensured that no one would be able to manufacture or sell the device without paying Alfred. While his first invention, a gasometer designed to measure liquids, earned him little money, it was an important first step. Over his lifetime, Alfred Nobel would earn over 350 patents in countries across the developed world.

In the 1840s and '50s, Immanuel likewise earned a series of patents for the land and sea mines that the Russian army was purchasing by the thousands. At his factory's peak, Immanuel Nobel employed over one thousand men, who all labored to construct the mines, which experts considered superior to any developed by Russians. The mines were primarily a defensive device, as Russia struggled to emerge victorious from a conflict known as the Crimean War.

Begun in 1853 during a dispute over the ownership of the key to the Church of the Nativity in Bethlehem, the Crimean War would eventually involve Turkey, France, and England, who united against Russia. Immanuel's sea mines were instrumental in protecting the Gulf of Finland from French and British forces at the cities of Kronshtadt, Tallinn (Revel), and Sveaborg. Although they did not destroy any ships, they were powerful enough to deter invasion.

Begun with a dispute over the ownership of the key to the Church of the Nativity, the Crimean War would eventually involve Russia, much of Europe and thousands of soldiers.

The Crimean War would last three years and cost thousands of lives, but in the end it accomplished little—although it did give Immanuel Nobel a taste of success, if only briefly. He even managed to finally pay off the debts from twenty years before.

The war did not end in Russia's victory, and after signing a treaty in Paris, the military refused to pay for the mines they'd ordered. Immanuel Nobel was left with a huge inventory and no buyers. He struggled to retool the factory for civilian use but was unsuccessful. He went broke very quickly. He returned to Sweden with Andriette and their youngest child, Emil.

His life was not as difficult as it had been in the 1830s. Ludvig managed to sell portions of the business and arrange lines of credit. He was able to set up a small income for his father and worked diligently to repay the debts Immanuel owed. He also changed the name of the company—a decision that probably did not please Immanuel, as "Nobel and Sons" became "The Brothers Nobel."

Alfred worked hard at his inventions; he knew that the right innovation would restore his family's fortune. He experimented with better explosives for the mines, but with the idea that even if the military's business faded, civilian uses would remain strong.

It was Alfred's old chemistry tutor, Nikolaj Zinin, who in 1855 demonstrated nitroglycerin to Albert. One single small explosion altered the Nobel family's fortune.

Zinin knew the Nobels were always in search of an explosive more powerful than gunpowder. In 1855 he showed them one. Nitroglycerin was discovered in 1847 by Italian chemist Ascanio Sobrero. The mixture of nitric acid, sulfuric acid, and glycerin produced an oily liquid that was both highly explosive and highly unstable. Sobrero himself developed a terror of the substance when during an experiment it blew up a test tube, leaving him with disfiguring facial scars. After that, Sobrero gave up nitroglycerin experiments.

Zinin emphasized the substance's danger to the Nobel brothers. Then he demonstrated its power. The professor dribbled a few drops of the liquid onto an anvil, and then struck it with a hammer. The blow created a tiny explosion and a sound like a gunshot. Only the liquid blew up, however: the anvil was undamaged. This suggested to Alfred that nitroglycerin could produce a focused explosion, one that could be utilized for a variety of civilian construction projects in which blowing up rocks and other obstacles could be useful. It could also help the military.

After his little demonstration, Zinin confessed to Alfred that he shared a popular belief: nitroglycerin's explosive ability would never be tamed.

Alfred had little patience for popular beliefs. Instead he embarked on a series of experiments designed to safely unlock nitro's power.

The challenge was how to detonate—or make explode—the nitroglycerin in a controlled manner. After a number of experiments, Alfred realized that the best way to utilize nitroglycerin was to combine it with something the Nobel family already had way too much of: gunpowder. By mixing the two explosives and then connecting them to a fuse and lighting it, Alfred was able to build a small but powerful bomb.

The three brothers began spending hours during the frigid winter outside on the frozen surface of the Neva Canal. In the beginning they simply filled some of their father's unsold mines with the mixture. They blew up a lot of ice. Unfortunately, as optimistic as he was, Alfred worried that the product was too unstable to be marketed.

Immanuel disagreed. By 1860, after getting Alfred's letters describing his nitro-gunpowder formula, Immanuel wrote back. He told his son that he had tested variations of the formula and come up with a combination that was both safer and more powerful than any Alfred had yet concocted. Taking credit for the invention, Immanuel told Alfred to start approaching Russian buyers.

Instead, in 1863 Alfred traveled to Sweden. What he found in the ramshackle shed behind his father's broken house was a disappointment. In a scathing letter, after he returned to Russia, Alfred said, "The result of my visit was a complete fiasco and proved that by then you had given up altogether the idea of glycerine powder, considering it impractical or not sufficiently developed."

Later in the same letter, Alfred concluded, "The only reason for indulgence on my part would be filial [son's] love, but in order for it to be maintained, it has to be mutual, and requires at least the same consideration as one owes to strangers."

Despite the sudden rift between father and son, Alfred's trip home had accomplished several things. Based on his father's experiments in the early 1860s, Alfred began using lead tubes instead of old mines. The tube shape would be an important component of his innovative use of nitro. He also realized something else during his summer in Sweden: "If one brings an insignificant amount of pyro[nitro]glycerine to a rapid explosion," he wrote, "that explosion must be forced by means of a detonation accompanied by heat to propagate the whole mass."

It was this concept—the idea of a primary and easily created first explosion followed by the second, main explosion—that revolutionized the technology.

In order to turn concept into reality, Alfred needed money. He managed to secure a small grant from the Swedish military. Unfortunately,

Alfred's attempt to do business with his native country was as unsuccessful as his father's had been three decades earlier.

In a demonstration at Karlsborg fortress, Alfred had packed a pig-iron bomb with a combination of 50 percent gunpowder and 50 percent nitroglycerin. He told the military observers to take cover.

Then he lit the fuse.

The explosion definitely made an impact. It scared the hardened officers half to death, and they refused to give Alfred any more funding. As far as they were concerned, the weapon was too dangerous for combat.

Discouraged but still convinced of nitroglycerin's potential benefits, Alfred changed his focus from military applications to civilian ones. He approached the Société de Crédit Mobilier, a French bank specializing in railroad loans. Alfred made a good pitch and the bankers agreed to loan him 100,000 francs—about 20,000 dollars.

It was quite a bit of money in 1861, but the bankers saw how, if properly controlled, the explosive could rip away at rock and other obstacles that railroad engineers encounter when laying track.

Financed, Alfred continued his experiments, eventually testing the theory he had described in the letter to his father.

"The real age of nitroglycerine began in 1864," Alfred later explained in another letter, "when an explosion with pure glycerine took place for the first time with the help of a very small charge of gunpowder."

The blasting, or detonating cap which Alfred invented, contained a small gunpowder charge attached to a fuse. The fuse was lit and the gunpowder exploded, "blasting" into the nitroglycerin below.

In his July 1864 patent application, Alfred wrote, "If the heat of the gunpowder can be imparted to nitroglycerine with the speed necessary for an explosion, then with the assistance of the impact and the pressure of developed gases, the ever greater heat developed in the nitroglycerine will, after a detonation impulse has been obtained, be able to sustain its own explosion."

Alfred had managed to do what no one before him had accomplished. He'd controlled nitroglycerin's power. However, he hadn't tamed it. Working with nitro was still dangerous. Learning just how dangerous would prove tragic for the Nobel family.

Despite its wartime applications, today dynamite is mainly used for civilian projects such as this mine in South Africa. The explosive has also helped level hillsides and create tunnels for railroads.

CHAPTER 5

A TRAGIC BENEFIT

No one needed to tell Alfred Nobel how dangerous nitroglycerin was. He already knew the stories of the maimed and the killed, but he suspected those victims had just been reckless. The key to working with nitroglycerin was a healthy respect for its power. With respect, it could be contained.

In 1863, Alfred patented his "method of preparing gunpowder for both blasting and shooting." The following year he patented his igniter, which incorporated a long, slow-burning fuse inside a cork, surrounded by fireproof material: the fuse is stuck inside a cap filled with gunpowder; the other end is lit. When the fuse ignites the tiny amount of gunpowder, a chain reaction is produced and the nitro blows up. For years, Alfred had been combining nitro and gunpowder, but only by separating them could he harness nitro's power. In the beginning he constructed his device in a glass tube; later, wooden tubes were used.

Alfred quickly interested mining companies in his new invention. In 1864 it was purchased by mine operators in Sweden and Germany. Although Alfred would eventually partner with some eight different companies located in nearly two dozen countries, in the early days his "factory" was the ramshackle shed on the back of his father's property in Sweden.

It was there that tragedy struck.

On September 3, 1864, Emil was working with several others in the shed. Alfred had trained his younger brother in the process of preparing nitro and felt comfortable leaving him alone.

A newspaper account from the time describes what happened. "People heard the violent sound of an explosion and saw a huge yellow flame rise straight up in the air. It was replaced within moments by an enormous pillar of smoke. . . . Most ghastly was the sight of the mutilated corpses strewn on the ground. Not only had the clothes been torn off but on some the head was missing and the flesh ripped off the bones. These formless masses of flesh and bone bore little resemblance to a human body."

Five people died that day. Among the dead, Emil. In an official inquiry, Immanuel stated what probably caused the explosion: "the tests my son was doing brought about a reaction that increased the temperature of the mixture to a temperature at which nitroglycerin explodes [around 180 degrees Celsius] . . . the cause of the accident was negligence."

In other words, Emil was to blame, not the nitroglycerin.

While in public he calmly fingered his dead son, privately Immanuel never recovered from the loss. Over the next few years he endured a series of paralyzing strokes. Alfred was saddened as well but pressed on with his experiments. The day after the explosion, Alfred, now the youngest Nobel, was back at work.

While the Nobels escaped criminal penalties, public outcry was enormous. Immanuel had never received permission from the authorities or his landlord to use the shed as a nitroglycerin factory, and after the accident Alfred was forced to relocate his facilities. Having to move his operations because of public fears would become very common for Alfred.

Many expected that this would be the incident that would permanently bankrupt the Nobels. They were wrong. Albert's product was in huge demand—even the Swedish government ordered it. On October 22, 1864, Alfred formed Nitroglycerine Aktiebolaget with J. W. Smitt, one of the wealthiest men in Sweden. Alfred and his father received half ownership of the company.

Throughout the remainder of Alfred's life, instead of licensing his product as other inventors did, he set up companies for which he was on the board of directors. This decision made him a very wealthy man by the time he was forty. It also guaranteed him a nomadic existence. He traveled throughout Europe, the United States, and other parts of the world, setting up new companies, protecting his patents, and generally behaving as much like a salesman or businessman as an inventor. "My homeland is wherever I work, and I work everywhere," Alfred wrote in a letter.

The events of late 1864 reflected what would become a constant issue for Alfred. While industry and governments alike begged for his product, some politicians and the people who supported them tried to enact laws limiting the manufacture, sale, and distribution of nitroglycerin.

Alfred, like his father, believed the problem with nitro was the negligence of some of the people who handled it. Workers who unpacked cans of it would spill the liquid accidentally. Sometimes they would use the yellow oil as a lubricant for wagon wheels or for their boots. This often provided a painful lesson in how *not* to treat nitro.

While Alfred believed his product was safe if handled with care, he also worked tirelessly to develop even safer alternatives.

Drawing on his background in chemistry, Alfred began to experiment with substances to make the nitro more stable, eliminating accidents. He figured instead of it being in a liquid, he could mix it with a solid. There is some evidence this was first suggested by Emil; regardless, Alfred's work mixing nitro with everything from paper pulp to ground charcoal was his younger brother's legacy.

Not until 1866 did he find a substance that absorbed the nitro without impeding its explosive power. Called kieselguhr earth, it was used to keep the cans of blasting oil protected during shipping. It was right under Alfred's nose, and it was perfect.

By combining 25 percent of the kieselguhr and 75 percent of the nitro, Alfred crafted a product that didn't get lumpy and could be shaped as desired. He mainly rolled it into stick form, and then in the testing process he dropped it into abandoned quarries and threw it against walls, but nothing caused it to explode. Yet when he used his patented blasting cap and lit its fuse, the new product exploded as well as nitro alone.

Alfred knew he had found the solution, but he did not want to call it anything that would remind people of nitroglycerin. Instead, he chose the Greek word for "power": *dynamis.* In 1866, Alfred began selling what would be his most famous invention: dynamite.

Nobel's money allowed him to construct the finest homes and laboratories, such as the one seen here. Throughout his entire life he never stopped inventing, and eventually he earned over 350 patents.

UNLUCKY IN LOVE

I n 1872, after suffering a slow and painful decline, Immanuel Nobel died. Through his last years he detailed a variety of inventions that, while they were never utilized, reflected his persistence. Immanuel was also able to observe the growing success of his son Alfred and of his product, dynamite.

Alfred traveled constantly. Unlike most inventors, he was not a wide-eyed dreamer with little business sense. Instead, Alfred could be ruthless when someone tried to sell one of his patented products without paying him.

The work ethic his father applauded when Alfred was a child paid off. By 1873, at the age of forty, he was a rich man. Alfred settled in his favorite city, Paris, and supervised the construction of a grand home on 53 Avenue Malakoff, featuring a winter garden covered by a glass wall and ceiling, a large formal dining room, a library, and, of course, a laboratory. (In 1881, Alfred would purchase an estate in Servan called Servan-Livery, north of Paris, for laboratory purposes. He would often stay there for several days when work built up).

The new home suited a man of means. So too did the carriage drawn by three horses, the butler, and the housekeeper. Alfred had everything, but he was very much alone.

In a letter typical of Alfred's moods in his middle age, he wrote, "I am spending almost the whole day at home, working. Time passes slowly because I feel very lonely. I have gotten out of the habit of participating in society life and am more and more out of contact with people."

The former Governess to a Baroness, Bertha von Suttner answered Nobel's advertisement for a secretary. When they met he quickly fell in love. Her departure did more damage to Nobel's heart than dynamite ever could.

Alfred Nobel's fame and financial success assured him a steady stream of invitations to the best parties and formal affairs society had to offer. Yet he usually declined. When he accepted, he would spend much of the evening alone in a corner, miserable and uncomfortable.

When it came to business and invention, Alfred was very successful—in 1875 he further improved explosive technology with a blasting gelatin.

The innovation came about after a cut finger kept Alfred awake one night and he applied some collodion to the wound. The substance, used in surgical bandages, worked for a while, but then flaked off.

At four A.M. he began to get some more, but instead considered its chemical composition. In his laboratory he thought about the collodion, which was dissolved cellulose in ether and alcohol, which after the ether evaporates leaves a lumpy mass. Alfred examined the cellulose. He dribbled nitro onto it. It dissolved.

He varied the proportions, eventually creating a blasting gelatin —or rubber dynamite. It was as safe as dynamite but could be used under water. Along with his 1887 invention ballistite, a smokeless explosive designed for the military, blasting gelatin and dynamite provided a source of constant and increasing income as Alfred grew older.

Nearly one hundred forty years after its development, dynamite continues to be widely used in demolition projects, including the leveling of this building to make way for a new Padres baseball stadium in San Diego.

Unfortunately the professional in business was an amateur with women. In 1876 he advertised for a secretary. It would be a highly demanding position, as Alfred's invoices, letters, and other paperwork arrived in five different languages. His employment ad ran in Vienna, Austria, a city he was visiting at the time. "Wealthy, highly educated elderly gentleman seeks lady of mature age, versed in languages as secretary and supervisor of household."

Thirty-three-year-old Countess Bertha Sofia Felitas Kinsky von Chinic und Tettau was the most qualified of the applicants. The daughter of an old and established Austrian family, Bertha's father was a poor military man, and so Bertha worked as a governess for the Baroness von Suttner's three daughters. It was a fine position, until she fell in love with Arthur von Suttner, the Baroness's twenty-six-year-old son.

Bertha needed a change. Alfred and Bertha wrote several letters back and forth, and he found himself increasingly drawn to Bertha's intelligence, wit, and grace. Even her upper-class background seemed to come through in her letters.

She arrived in Paris in 1876, and Alfred was immediately struck by her regal beauty. Bertha was equally stunned—the "elderly gentleman" was only forty-three! Still, as she later wrote her mother, "Because of all the letters we had exchanged, we did not feel as though we were strangers to each other."

The two conversed as equals. Alfred told her in a letter that he hoped to "invent a substance or machine so frightfully effective and devastating that it would forever make wars altogether impossible." He even showed her a few poems he had written.

Bertha, for her part, recorded in her diary: "To speak with him about the world and people, about life and art, about problems of the moment or eternal problems was an exquisite pleasure."

Although middle-aged and wealthy, there are few accounts of Alfred ever having a girlfriend by the time he met Bertha. So maybe his mistaking her interest for passion was understandable. Over an expensive lunch, Alfred shyly asked if Bertha's "heart was taken."

Her response devastated the lonely inventor. While she tried to be as gentle as possible, she told Alfred that she had only recently broken her engagement to Arthur. She was still very much in love.

The next day business pulled Alfred from Paris. A week later he returned to find Bertha gone. She had paid for her hotel room by selling a family heirloom—when the hotel manager told her Alfred expected to be billed for her stay, she refused to allow it.

Bertha married Arthur von Suttner on June 12, 1876, without his parents' blessing. Alfred would stay in touch with Bertha for the rest of his life.

Heartbroken and vulnerable, four months after Bertha's wedding, Alfred began a fifteen-year relationship with Sofie Hess, a gorgeous but manipulative twenty-year-old who worked at a florist shop. The couple never married, but Alfred financed her increasingly expensive lifestyle, while frequently criticizing her lack of education or breeding in the letters he wrote to her. It was, in modern terms, a very unhealthy relationship.

In 1891 it ended when Alfred learned that Sofie was pregnant with another man's child.

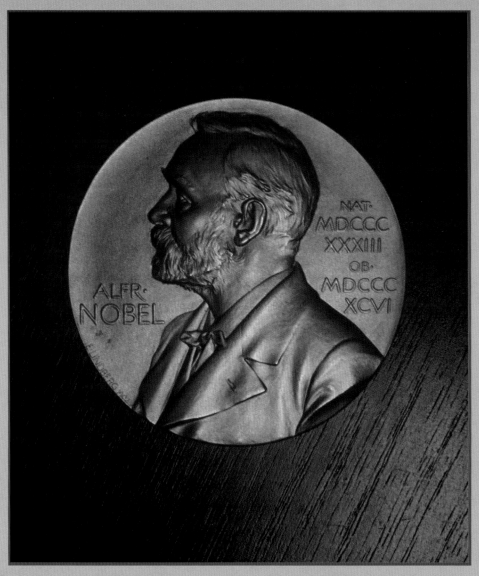

The legacy of a man afraid of how he'd be remembered, this prize is truly Alfred's "noblest" achievement.

CHAPTER 7

TESTAMENT

Brooding and increasingly depressed, Alfred Nobel's dark mood was hardly improved by the publication of an inaccurate French obituary. Incorrectly describing Alfred's death, the newspaper slammed the reclusive inventor for the deadliness of his inventions. Indeed, just seven years before, dynamite was used to assassinate Czar Alexander II in St. Petersburg, Alfred's adolescent home.

Alfred's inventions, along with part ownership in brother Robert's Russian oil company, Branobel (one of the largest in the world), made Alfred a millionaire several times over. Such wealth in the late nineteenth century was very rare. Once, when a servant of his was getting married, he asked her what she wanted. "As much as Monsieur Nobel himself earns in one day," she replied. Impressed with her gumption, Alfred gave her a check for over 40,000 francs—today over one hundred thousand dollars.

While he was generous, Alfred wanted to do more. He wanted a legacy. He did not have any children, and he did not think dynamite the proper remembrance.

By 1895 a dispute with the French government led him to settle in San Remo, a scenic town on Italy's Mediterranean coast. It was there that he drew up his will—a document in his own writing headed *Testament.*

He ordered that his estate—then worth close to ten million dollars—be invested in "stable securities" such as interest bearing bonds, "the annual interest on which shall be awarded as prizes to those persons who during the previous year have rendered the greatest services to mankind."

Along with the Peace Prize ceremony in Oslo, Norway, December's Nobel Prize Ceremony in Stockholm, Sweden receives coverage from newspapers, magazines and television stations across the globe. 2002 Peace Prize Winner former President Jimmy Carter made front-page headlines.

The prize money was to be divided into five parts: the physics, chemistry, physiology or medicine, and literature awards would be given in his native Sweden. The fifth award—the Nobel Peace Prize—was for "the person who has done the most or the best work for the brotherhood of the nations, the abolishment or reduction of standing armies, as well as for the establishment and spread of peace congresses." It was to be awarded by a committee in Norway.

On December 10, 1896, three days after suffering a cerebral hemorrhage, Alfred Nobel died. Neither family nor friends were by his side. His death was witnessed only by those on his payroll.

The testament he had drawn up led to the kind of obituary he had hoped for. On January 2, 1897, a newspaper in Stockholm called Nobel's testament "a gift to mankind intended to further its development and promote its welfare, as well as to serve purely idealistic purposes—

probably the most magnificent one of its kind that a private person had the desire and the ability to make."

Although this opinion was not shared by everyone—its "international" flavor angered Swedish nationalists—most were impressed. Because of legal complexities (including the King of Sweden fighting the Peace Prize's awarding in Norway), Alfred Nobel's last will and testament was not implemented until December 31, 1900, when the Nobel Foundation received 31,225,000 Swedish crowns—almost seven million dollars.

Every October the awards are announced. On December 10 the Peace Prize is awarded in Oslo, Norway. The other five prizes (economics was added in 1968) are given out the same day in Stockholm. The prizes are considered one of the highest honors anyone can achieve—and by 1996 the money given with the prize exceeded one million dollars.

Sometimes they are controversial. The 1994 shared Peace Prize given to Yassar Arafat, Shimon Peres, and Yitzhak Rabin for their Israeli-Palestine peace accord was widely criticized. Still, the prize is the pinnacle of achievement and has been for over a century, thanks to Alfred Nobel's foresight.

In 1905, Bertha von Suttner, the woman Alfred loved and lost, won the Nobel Peace Prize for her work promoting world peace and for her novel *Lay Down Your Arms: The Autobiography of Martha von Tilling.* Many believe that despite marrying another, her influence on Alfred was part of the reason he included the prize for peace in his testament.

NOBEL PRIZE WINNERS

Winners, 1998–2002
(For a complete listing of all Nobel Prizes, 1901–Present, see www.nobel.se/nobel/index.html)

Nobel Prize in Physics
Awarded by the Royal Swedish Academy of Sciences
2002   Raymond Davis Jr., Masatoshi Koshiba, Riccardo Giacconi
2001   Eric A. Cornell, Wolfgang Ketterle, Carl E. Wieman
2000   Zhores I. Alferov, Herbert Kroemer, Jack S. Kilby
1999   Gerardus 't Hooft, Martinus J.G. Veltman
1998   Robert B. Laughlin, Horst L. Störmer, Daniel C. Tsui

Nobel Prize in Chemistry
Awarded by the Royal Swedish Academy of Sciences
2002   John B. Fenn, Koichi Tanaka, Kurt Wüthrich
2001   William S. Knowles, Ryoji Noyori, K. Barry Sharpless
2000   Alan J. Heeger, Alan G. MacDiarmid, Hideki Shirakawa
1999   Ahmed H. Zewail
1998   Walter Kohn, John A. Pople

Nobel Prize in Physiology or Medicine
Awarded by the Nobel Assembly at Karolinska Institutet
2002   Sydney Brenner, H. Robert Horvitz, John E. Sulston
2001   Leland H. Hartwell, R. Timothy (Tim) Hunt, Sir Paul M. Nurse
2000   Arvid Carlsson, Paul Greengard, Eric R. Kandel
1999   Günter Blobel
1998   Robert F. Furchgott, Louis J. Ignarro, Ferid Murad

Nobel Prize in Literature
Awarded by the Swedish Academy
2002   Imre Kertész
2001   V.S. Naipaul
2000   Gao Xingjian
1999   Günter Grass
1998   José Saramago

Nobel Prize in Peace
Awarded by the Norwegian Nobel Committee
2002   Jimmy Carter
2001   United Nations (U.N.), Kofi Annan
2000   Kim Dae-jung
1999   Médecins Sans Frontières
1998   John Hume, David Trimble

The Bank of Sweden Prize in Economic Sciences in Memory of Alfred Nobel (since 1968)
Awarded by the Royal Swedish Academy of Sciences
2002   Daniel Kahneman, Vernon L. Smith
2001   George A. Akerlof, A. Michael Spence, Joseph E. Stiglitz
2000   James J. Heckman, Daniel L. McFadden
1999   Robert A. Mundell
1998   Amartya Sen

CHRONOLOGY

1833   Alfred Bernhard Nobel is born on October 21 in Stockholm, Sweden

1837   Father Immanuel accepts a job offer in Turku, Finland, leaving his family in Stockholm

1842   Alfred moves with his mother and two older brothers to St. Petersburg, Russia, where his father has been working for several years

1849   Alfred travels to Sweden, England, Germany, Italy, France, and finally the United States, where he works for American inventor John Ericsson

1854   Alfred returns to St. Petersburg

1860   Alfred tests a mixture of gunpowder and nitroglycerin on the Neva Canal

1863   Alfred returns to Sweden and earns his first patent for his "method of preparing gunpowder for both blasting and shooting"

1864   Earns patent for Nobel igniter; the shed Alfred uses for experiments explodes, killing five people, including his youngest brother, Emil

1866   Alfred stabilizes nitro by mixing it with kieselguhr and begins selling dynamite; he again travels to the United States, asserting his patent rights and establishing continuous production of dynamite; earns his first British patent

1867   Earns British patent for dynamite

1868   Earns U.S. patent for dynamite

1870   Builds dynamite factory in Paulilles, France

1873   Has a large house built in Paris

1875   Invents "rubber dynamite," a safer blasting gelatin

1876   Falls in loves with Bertha Kinsky, who breaks his heart by marrying a baron; begins relationship with a twenty-year-old florist's clerk, Sofie Hess

1879   Branobel, a Russian oil company owned by Alfred and his brother Robert, formed in Russia

1884   Invents ballistite, a smokeless gunpowder

1887   Earns patent in France for ballistite

1888   A French newspaper erroneously reports Alfred's death

1896   Alfred Nobel dies from a cerebral hemorrhage on December 10; his will, signed November 27, 1895, establishes a trust fund for the Nobel Prize

EVENTS IN ALFRED NOBEL'S LIFETIME

1833	Slavery abolished throughout British Empire
1836	Battle of the Alamo fought by Americans seeking independence from Mexico; Swedish shipbuilder John Ericsson patents screw propellers to power ships
1837	Samuel Morse invents the telegraph
1839	France's Louis Daguerre develops the daguerreotype process, an early form of photography
1845	Sugary desert made of gelatin is invented; it will eventually be made famous as Jell-O
1847	Italian chemist Ascanio Sobrero discovers nitroglycerin
1848	Revolt in France leads to rebellions throughout Europe, including in Italy, Hungary, and Germany; U.S.-Mexico War ends, with Mexico losing claims to Texas, California, Arizona, New Mexico, Utah, and Nevada
1850	During the California Gold Rush, Levi Strauss begins selling the first jeans
1853-1856	The Crimean War is waged between Russia and the countries of England, France, and the Ottoman Empire (Turkey)
1860-1865	The U.S. Civil War is waged
1862	Étienne Lenoir builds the first automobile with an internal combustion engine; Abraham Lincoln signs the Emancipation Proclamation, freeing slaves as of January 1, 1863
1865	Abraham Lincoln is assassinated
1869	In Utah the Union Pacific and Central Pacific Railroad meet as the first track across the United States is completed
1876	Mark Twain (Samuel Clemens) publishes *The Adventures of Tom Sawyer*; Alexander Graham Bell patents the telephone
1877, 1880	Thomas Edison invents the phonograph and the first electric lightbulb

FURTHER READING

FOR YOUNG ADULTS:

Ash, Russell. *Factastic Millennium Facts.* New York: DK Publishing, 1999.

Culligan, Judy. *Scientists and Inventors* (Macmillan Profiles). New York: Macmillan Library Reference, 1998.

Traub, Carol G. *Philanthropists and their Legacies.* Minneapolis: The Oliver Press, 1997.

ON THE INTERNET:

Alfred Nobel—Man Behind the Prizes
www.nobel.se/nobel/alfred-nobel/index.html

Nobel in Print
www.wfu.edu/users/esteas0/print.htm

WORKS CONSULTED:

Bergengren, Erik. *Alfred Nobel: The Man and His Work.* London: Thomas Nelson and Sons, 1960.

Christman, Henry M., editor. *Walt Whitman's New York.* New York: The Macmillan Company, 1963.

Evlanoff, Michale, and Marjorie Fluor. *Alfred Nobel: The Loneliest Millionaire.* Los Angeles: The Ward Ritchie Press, 1969.

Fant, Keene. *Alfred Nobel: A Biography.* New York: Arcade Publishing, 1991.

Gray, Tony. *Champions of Peace.* Birmingham, England: Paddington Press, 1976.

Sohlman, Ragnar. *The Legacy of Alfred Nobel.* Translated in English. London: The Bodley Head, 1983.

Sohlman, Ragner, and Henrik Schuck. *Nobel: Dynamite and Peace.* New York: Cosmopolitan Book Corporation, 1929.

Withey, Lynne. *Grand Tours and Cook's Tours: A History of Leisure Travel, 1750–1915.* New York: William Morrow and Company, 1997.

GLOSSARY

Cellulose	(SELL-yih-lows) Shapeless fiber in plant tissues used to make paper, explosives, and textiles.
Detonate	(DEH-te-nayt) To make something explode.
Dynamite	(DYE-ne-might) Alfred Nobel's 1866 invention combining nitro-glycerin and absorbent material, usually produced in sticks, and used as an explosive.
Extirpate	(EK-stir-payt) to destroy completely; wipe out
Fuse	(fyooz) Length of material that can be lit to carry flame to an explosive.
Indulgence	(in-DULL-jents) the state of gratifying one's own desires or wishes.
Igniter	(ig-NIGHT-er) Device used to start a fire or explosion.
Nitroglycerin	(nye-troh-GLISS-er-in) Highly explosive oily yellow liquid.
Patent	(PAT-nt) Government protection ensuring that the inventor has the sole right to his invention for a period of time.
Propagate	(PROP-eh-gayt) To spread or multiply.
Respite	(RES-pit) a period of rest or relief
Testament	(TEST-eh-ment) Legal document that explains how a written will's property will be distributed.
Thwarted	(THWORT-ed) to run counter to, or against; effectively oppose or turn away.

INDEX